W9-AAL-657

Season of the Second Thought

WISCONSIN POETRY SERIES

Ronald Wallace, Series Editor

Season of the Second Thought

Lynn Powell

The University of Wisconsin Press

The University of Wisconsin Press
1930 Monroe Street, 3rd Floor
Madison, Wisconsin 53711-2059
uwpress.wisc.edu

3 Henrietta Street, Covent Garden
London WCE 8LU, United Kingdom
eurospanbookstore.com

Printed in the United States of America

This book may be available in a digital edition.

Library of Congress Cataloging-in-Publication Data

Names: Powell, Lynn, 1955- author.
Title: Season of the second thought / Lynn Powell.
Other titles: Wisconsin poetry series.
Description: Madison, Wisconsin : The University of Wisconsin Press, [2017] |
          Series: Wisconsin poetry series | Includes bibliographical references.
Identifiers: LCCN 2017010436 | ISBN 9780299315344 (pbk. : alk. paper)
Subjects: | LCGFT: Poetry.
Classification: LCC PS3566.O83255 S43 2017 | DDC 811/.54—dc23
LC record available at https://lccn.loc.gov/2017010436

For Anna-Claire and Jesse,
who help me look more closely
and see more clearly

CONTENTS

Three

ACKNOWLEDGMENTS

My thanks to the editors of the following publications, where these poems first appeared, sometimes in slightly different form:

American Literary Review: "Gale Force Hymn"

Appalachian Heritage: "Alberta Clipper"

Artful Dodge: "October Edge"

The Bellingham Review: "Driftings at Anchor" and "Feedback for the Muse"

An Easy Gravity: Poems for Elton Glaser (University of Akron Press, 2008): "Master Class"

FIELD: "Duet for Ecclesiastes and Dutch Weather" and "Indian Summer"

From the Finger Lakes: A Poetry Anthology (Cayuga Lake Books, Ithaca, 2016): "In the Thin-Lipped, Purifying Weather"

Georgia Review: "On the Silver Anniversary of a Heartbreak" and "A Scherzo for Sadness"

Poetry: "Kind of Blue"

Rivendell: "July's Proverb" and "The Moon Rising"

Shenandoah: "Fragments of a Lost Gospel," "Love Poem from the Wrong Side of the Rain," and "Tantrum, with Mistletoe"

Southern Poetry Review: "Vernal Knowledge"

Tiferet: "Woman in Blue Reading a Letter"

The following poems were reprinted in anthologies:

> *From the Finger Lakes: A Poetry Anthology* (Cayuga Lake Books, Ithaca, 2016): "July's Proverb" and "Love Poem from the Wrong Side of the Rain"

> *The Norton Introduction to Literature*, 10th ed. (W. W. Norton, 2010): "Kind of Blue"

> *The Southern Poetry Anthology*, vol. 3, *Contemporary Appalachia* (Texas Review Press, 2010): "Fragments of a Lost Gospel," "Indian Summer," and "Kind of Blue"

> *The Southern Poetry Anthology*, vol. 6, *Tennessee* (Texas Review Press, 2013): "July's Proverb"

"At the Equinox" first appeared on the website of *Spark and Echo Arts* (October, 2013).

I am grateful for the support of a Literature Fellowship from the National Endowment for the Arts for 2007 and for Individual Excellence Awards in poetry from the Ohio Arts Council for 2004 and 2014.

My special thanks to Tom Dukes and Elton Glaser, for their crucial feedback on every poem in this book and for helping my voice stay Southern in northern Ohio.

And to my husband, Dan Stinebring, for the life we share on land and water, a life that makes poetry possible.

One

Kind of Blue

Not Delft or
delphinium, not Wedgewood
among the knickknacks, not wide-eyed chicory
evangelizing in the devil strip—

  But way on down in the moonless
  octave below midnight, honey,
  way down where you can't tell cerulean from teal.

Not Mason jars of moonshine, not
waverings of silk, not the long-legged hunger
of a heron or the peacock's
iridescent id—

  But Delilahs of darkness, darling,
  and the muscle of the mind
  giving in.

Not sullen snow slumped
against the garden, not the first instinct of flame,
not small, stoic ponds, or the cold derangement
of a jealous sea—

  But bluer than the lips of Lazarus, baby,
  before Sweet Jesus himself could figure out
  what else in the world to do but weep.

Alberta Clipper

March strides in like a woman scorned—
she hates the lukewarm look of the sun,
its pale, obligatory touch.
You can't have what you don't want, she snaps.

In her fierce fleece, with her manicure of ice,
she's in no mood for mockingbirds
whinging on about the moon's spilt milk,
no sucker for the bait and switch of dandelions,
and she's had it with the buds, all that private eagerness
for histrionic pink.

She keeps what's tender cringing underground,
and what should be tears, she starves
into a reticence of white.
Whoever still believes in spring will have to stare her down.

Feedback for the Muse

Thanks, I guess, for the souped-up sunset,
the daisies and their two-bit oracles, the picked-over
sweets with the dark and nutty gone.
But could we ink in soon a meeting of the minds?
It's words I'm wanting here.

If I were a Greek, I'd gladly read a steamy entrail.
If I were a zealot, I'd rummage through
apocrypha and zodiacs to catch your drift.
If I were postmodern, I'd theorize you don't exist,
and call your bluff.

But you know me: I compost tea leaves and call a star a star.
I think a thought doesn't count till I can taste it on the tongue.

Remember what we promised?
Kiss and tell it like nobody else.

So don't bother sending trifles dredged
from the rock bottom of your heart.
Or roses blazing some bloody message—like flares
at the edge of a wrecked desire.

No Proust, No Stevens, No Nietzsche

1

What got thought elsewhere, stayed elsewhere—
except for mail sent to our Chattanooga mailbox,
galvanized at the end of a new dead end.

I watched for the mailman's car from the perch
of my Schwinn Starlet, or from the porch if *the devil
was beating his wife* (the sun bright in spite

of an outburst of rain). On good days: the "family
bulletin" from Uncle Duck—cigar-haunted onionskin
with smudged news of Harlan and Georgia,

floozy jokes, and gibes at screwloose yankees.
And on best days: the only novels I knew to read,
fresh from the refiner's fire of *Reader's Digest*.

2

We got close enough to kiss, but then
that boy stood up and forced a different laying on
of hands, for he knew God was everywhere

and especially in East Tennessee.
Repent! and he *meant* it, looking down on me
with the seasoned glare of an exorcist.

I glared back but let him do
what he was going to do to my harlot soul.
In his grandma's knick-knacked

living room, there were no swine, though,
no serpents, not even hot coals in the Franklin stove—
no place for that demon to go but further in.

3

Barbeque and Jack Daniels for the famous poet,
which I suppose they thought was clever that far north
of the Mason-Dixon Line.

And I was introduced, fresh from the hills,
as poetic kin. *I know what I'd like to do with that
young thang*, he winked to his peers.

I hated how prettily I flushed, how my words
froze, but I was Southern, startled, and young enough
to laugh it off. In time I learned to chalk him up

to another weak man in exile—though not
so far gone as a girl in the small boat of her thought,
adrift in the gale force of language.

Woman in Blue Reading a Letter

after Vermeer

No window, just an assumption
that light must come from somewhere
and it's best to turn your face to it.

Velvets and austerities she's loved
now gently hem her in—two upright chairs,
a wedge of tapestry and table, the far wall's
opalescent whitewash and iron gleam
of the bar weighting down the world behind her,
its thick line aimed through her chest—
while gold is sparse and magnetized, like insight,
to what is hard, pearls or bits of brass.

That faded parchment in the background
maps an older version of uplift,
rift, and deluge: cataclysms
now inhabited and named. She is larger,
closer, the cloud-smeared blue of her jacket
and the furrowed ochre of her skirt so sturdy
she's lost the need for shadow.
She bears her darkness all on her own back.

Still, it takes both hands to steady the slender paper
she holds level with her heart.
Nothing's brighter than the blank
back of the page, the hot silence
just this side of revelation.
Only she knows what words she peers down into,
what black penmanship incites the flush on her face—

lines that find their mark and leave her
reading on and on in unrelenting light.

Love Poem from the Wrong Side of the Rain

What would April do? Tease hidden
meanings from the bulbs, raise the stakes
and double my entendres, and bet
all my roses on the bottom line.

But it's the season of embarrassed trees,
the modest charms of leaf rot and briar
and hawk scat thawing on the muddy path:
skinny March at an earnest latitude.

So tell me, Muse: where around here might a woman
find a little flint and tinder,
some figure of feisty speech, a correlative for kisses
that would make a grown man weep if she put it
all on the table and headed out
for good into the long-stemmed rain?

Fragments of a Lost Gospel

1

April at flood stage, and the mercury
rising to the occasion—the blind pond healed
of its cataract of ice; the sky's
white hemorrhage stopped.

And who was there when the stone
of winter rolled away?
A glossolalia of geese.
Magdalenas in the orchard repenting of their nakedness.

2

No suet in the feeder. No chime in the wind.
The loose magnolia singed by frost. And nothing
for me again in the blue satchel of the mailman.

And my own heart stubborn as a love letter
written in the passive voice.

3

What is this shrub with flowers in its hair?

Country cousin to the rose,
slut in a white dress,
it flatters the barbed wire, then throws
itself at the trees.

Along my path, there is a throng of it—
chaste fragrance with a hungry reach,
and soft, ambivalent thorns.

4

That mockingbird can aim its song at me,
batter its bravado against the open pane.
It can gossip to the grapevine,
mooch the music of the sparrow, festoon
the silent pillars of the dark.

But that bird can't argue me out of my loneliness.
It can't filibuster
the tongue-tied stamina of my grief.

5

The green's turned to a familiar passage.
I set aside my shears and bow
my mind to the *lectio*.
What other way is there for me to know my heart?

If I listen, I can hear the small, crimson
creed of the cardinal.

If I wait, I can watch my shadow
wade into the light.

6

The yard's still head over heels in purple.
But once it is plucked, what exactly
can you do with a violet?

Place it on a page,
and send the weight of half the language bearing down.

7

The sky has a mind so clear it can read itself.
I wish I had a mind like that:
one sharp-shinned thought at home on the updraft.

Down here, the wind stirs up a dry
dervish in the unsown field—a godforsaken god
scuffing her heel in the dust.

Gale Force Hymn

So this is the way the day ends:
      with a gnash of teeth and harrumphs
from heaven, a black mood smiting

the clueless blue. Clouds snag on the hills
      and drag a downpour like torn lace.
Trees writhe like Pentecostals.

But it's too late to coax God to be good,
      too late to grovel with tears or hosannas:
nothing swerves the will of a whirlwind.

It lifts up the loose and unhinged, bangs
      them down the street, hurls them at the helpless
glass, till the panicked air

sickens and sirens wail for steeples
      and strip joints and trailers strung out
along the soft shoulders of secondary roads—

and nothing's blesséd but the cockroach,
      the mole in the ground, the immortal
roots of the mean buckthorn.

Slow Elegy from Afar

Then the Lord answered Job out of the whirlwind:
... *Where were you when I laid the foundation of the earth?*

What glitch in the genes created shame?
God, the oldest scapegoat, usually gets the rap.

But why would the maker of that granite island—
glacier-polished nub of a Precambrian peak,
with an osprey perched, bellyful of fish, in a wind-bent pine,
the gibbous moon floating up, and the evening star,
on cue, surfacing in a lavender sky—why
would the God of that cold beauty
contrive a hall of mirrors in a human mind?

On our last long walk five springs ago, we sparred, gingerly.
You were a brilliant believer; I had come to believe
that cruelty was the only sin—with the caveat
that cruelty could also be the secret name of subtler sins.
Everything else, I argued, *is the blundering of a desire
to be known, loved, or safe. We make mistakes
and know ourselves.*

I could see your young, tired face tighten.

So I tried a different tack—
Don't take the perfect so personally.
Don't take shame so much to heart.

Why did you suffer? And why did you leave
your suffering to those you loved?

I can't gird my loins again against my childhood God,
that God with a clipboard and swift red pen.

So I reread Job, and watch the waves wash,
and aim to wash away, the granite shore.
They paraphrase the whirlwind.

As do the oriole that slings her hammock nest
along the path we walked, the doe in the close woods
wary for her fawn, the thunderhead and the downpour,
the firefly galaxies in the blackest field of night,
the forsythia festive once again beside your grave.

July's Proverb

The shortest distance between what's gone and what's to come
is you. But that's neither here
nor there to the rabbit, plush
and quick in the rainsoft grass,
or to that taut bird, hotwired for song.

The noon sky acts as if nothing mauve has ever happened.
Clouds go on and on about the weather.
And soon enough, the delicate
hypocrisy of winter—snow falling all over itself
to wish you weren't here.

There's no wisdom in the wind vane,
and no help in that daytime moon,
slow, half-hearted, besieged by blue. Yet the mind
keeps watching from its shade of words—
the mind and its archangel, the flesh.

Indian Summer

1

Dawn bailing out the sluggish dark as if
the day still might right itself in the wake
of the equinox—

in this season of the second thought,
with its clear blue falsetto sky and flashbacks to crimson.
Like spring, in a bolder key.

2

By now, each day's an anniversary of something—
a first or final touch, or kiss, or blow . . .

back to a split-level girlhood in the Appalachian South:
pom-poms and curlers and a red-leather Bible
embossed with my gold name.

I left home with a pedigree of Pentecost
and *Do unto others as you would have them do unto you.*
Which I did, in my earnest and wanton way.

3

Last night a cake on fire and plastic cups of champagne.

Today, it's drunken bees in a wheelbarrow of windfall rot,
and poison, tit for tat, on the poison ivy.

Think what you wish for, they cheered
as I blew the decades out—
think, think.

4

A storm front slips across another state line,
moist touch to the cheek of the rain-starved air.

And who could begrudge the geese and the asters,
the last field of corn shriveling in the October sun?

Yet I keep my eye on the conscientious oak
and, closer, the slender limbs of the locust,

trifling with the wind through my bay window glass.

5

The pang that passes understanding—
and, all morning, a cello's mahogany grief.

Where else but in this small white room can I weep,
not wronged or widowed,
forgiver or forgiven?

Outside in the breezy yard, the sun blusters on,
and hard buds tighten on vines—
little think tanks,
with their far-fetched scenarios of pink.

6

The days slide round again to this one, drawn back
as if to the scene of a crime,
and the heart still sifting through the evidence.

What do you mean by "my"? chides the wind,
unraveling the maples with its Buddhist hands.

7

The sky shakes out a scribble of starlings,
then erases them
from its lavender slate.
Why are they more real once I want to tell you of them?

Grief, love, anger—which would I send
as a swoop of starlings over shattered fields?

And beyond them, in a nonchalance of dusk, the moon
full again and face to face
with the unwavering light of Venus.

Two

October Edge

Mapless and skidding again on a backroad
prickly with teasels and sumac and skeletons
of lace, I glimpse a pink non sequitur:
a winged woman on the stoop
of a whitewashed church, glancing up
from an opened book and lifting
her opened hand—

but I will not brake today for grace,
I round the reckless curve, past pumpkins
with no faces forced yet on them, past
bins and barrels of crimson wholesale fruit,
past tombstones disheveled in the drizzle
staggering after their long-lost
ballast of grief—

the blurred signs vanishing
like everything else in the hindsight horizon,
and the black tires taking my incendiary heart
farther, faster, out past the charred trunks of the maples,
those miles of martyrs with feet
held fast to the banked flames
of their own making.

Species of Idolatry

Like a thorn in the side of a great museum—
this small, dull painting, lodged
in a gallery of black-hatted burghers and their flashy still lifes.
It recounts a day their rabble roused and smashed
each graven thing, fixing the errors made
in God's good name with a rash of their own.

With perfect perspective (circa 1630), its church provides
a field guide to that *Beeldenstorm*:
one believer noosing a saint's stone throat,
one lugging God's mother to the door like a stiffened corpse,
two toppling Sweet Jesus from his wormwood cross.
A few, with ladders, whitewash the frescoes,
while the fiercest lash out at a Last Judgment, hacking up the naked
whether destined for rapture's creamy clouds
or the Boschian obscenities of hell.
"It was a savage day in Dutch history," proclaims the placard.

Streaming to the Golden Age, no one pauses
by this faded scene of the righteous running riot.
And why should they—when zealots now, on a billion tiny screens,
shout down the seeker and the skeptic, pump their fists
for purges, or make so much bloodier mayhem
in their own instant image?

On the Silver Anniversary of a Heartbreak

You're not the *you* you used to be—
even my poems don't speak of you now.

      I make no image in your image.

Once, you could sway that crowd of tattered asters
into wild and purple thoughts.

      Should I pine for that grief or weep for my old tears?

There's no pang in *sangfroid*,
no sass in the healed heart.

      Once, our pond lay belly up to the light.

Here, it's another synonym for silence.
And the dayshift moon goes on about its business

      and never once recalls your name.

Master Class

for Elton Glaser

The wind stays up all night and edits
November's rough draft of the yard.

It sees right through the minds
of the star magnolia and the sidewalk maple

and rips out the rot and the deadwood,
the dull leaves hanging on for a last sip of sap.

By morning, the ground's cluttered with culls
for the brush pile, and there's a widow-maker to hack

and drag and hide along the margin.
Oh, I could build one helluva fire with all these flaws

I never noticed, hovering, summerlong,
inside the glib green consensus of the trees.

In the Thin-Lipped, Purifying Weather

Cold rain, zealous wind, and cobalt churned
to froth and whitewashed sky:
that's what an easy season always comes to.
The great lake hardens, its piers
reaching out into the deep for no good reason.
The sand comes clean.
And the park, that soft spot
for chess and Pabst and moonlit trysts,
gets overwrought with iron and clanged shut.

So who cares?
Nobody but me and that dog—
cruising the edge with a cold black nose, hungry
for a bit of sweet or grease, a skinny-haunched mutt
Caravaggio would have loved.
He whines at empty bins, sniffs
at the puzzle of gate and lock, digs in ground
that won't give an inch, till there's nothing to do but
hold up his head and head down the beach, the wind
so wild he trots a sideways jig
to aim himself straight—
our tracks a fugue of left and wrong and right.

Postcard to the Muse

Wish you were still here.

But I can read between the missing lines:
you've stuffed your silk enjambments
in your attaché and hightailed south.

Winter's on each corner now, hawking
the fixed ideas of the trees and littering
the town with apocalyptic tracts,

dry testimonials to frost and wind.
Geese fall into line. Ragged maples
give up their last gold mite.

And I keep trying to believe in you—
though God knows who you're shacked up with,
rhyming sassafras with sweetgum

and taking moonlight way too personally.
There's nothing to report, nothing new
beneath this dingy sun.

Only hunters in loud orange, loaded and ready
to cull the grace that ransacked my garden,
to snipe at the mistletoe lodged

in the high, clear mind of the oak.

In Another Aftermath

The Massacre of the Innocents, an altarpiece by Cornelis van Haarlem after the 1573 Spanish siege of Haarlem

After such pain, what else could you paint?
After siege and starvation, surrender and revenge,
who needs a crust of pearls

on the hem of a meticulous Mary?
The holy toddler with a nibbled pomegranate
or a goldfinch on his finger?

And so, "this great confusion of naked child-killers," this
vortex of muscle, this opulent cruelty, these honed heroic men
who rip plump babies from their mothers' arms

and slit their throats like pigs. The babies cool
to white on cobblestone, as the mothers' eyes roll
back into their heads, demonic with anguish.

In a different age or republic, those little boys
might be busy cherubs, Cupids bothered by honeybees,
or messiahs on the laps of their straight-faced moms.

But here, in the next millennium,
in a city besieged by tourists for its tulips
and its art, on a soft day of early snow,

in a hushed room of Edens
and angels and that sad man caught again
in the crosshairs of a crucifix—

they are flesh incarnate,
a slaughter of *only begottens*, the savage news
that won't stop arriving.

A Scherzo for Sadness

Snow is making light of the dark trees.
And in a snow-lit room, a violin

is trying to climb its way out of the music, out
of a sudden surfeit of bleak beauty.

And what, today, are you, my heart?
Some days you act like a young woman

wearing, in April, heavy wool
deployed against her own soft heat.

Some days you smash through hours
like a lost deer panicking into glass.

Some days you believe in nothing but
a hairpin thought, or the thin line

where heaven and earth keep trying to touch.
Why not forgive yourself those tears

and your honest trespasses?
Remember how miserly the perfect are,

both the cynic and the saint: all that love
they could have wasted gone to waste.

The Argument for Zero

Desire is in the details—
that's the trouble with a green season.

Who can quibble with crocus or reason
with a backyard tree riddled with cherries?
Who can mentor magnolias

while they're dropping pink and blatant hints?
They complicate the moonlight;
they lure the sunlight into shade.

Thus the guiding principle of January,
and all its lovely corollary
ghosts of tears.

Calmed and cold, they know how to
salve a broken orchard, soothe
a prickly garden, smother

the last wild quandary of the lavender.

Voice Overs

Remembering violets he had murmured
to the décolletage of Berthe Morisot,
Manet demurred, *A painter can say*
all he wants with fruit or flowers.

And Hopper, who could put light up against a wall
better than anybody, chided,
If you could say it in words,
there would be no reason to paint.

But what would they say with these ruined
and brittle shades, with this haggard
palette of winter and wind?

∽

All night, a sift of silence.
Today the path is pretty for the smother of white,
like everything bristly in my childhood:
If you can't say anything nice, don't—

Though reticence, too, has its problems:
a mind muffled in metaphor,
a chaste touch that backfires into lust,
the right line that ends
again on the wrong thought.

∽

I envy the ones who head to the tropics and hang
with hibiscus and bougainvillea, bohemians
who know how to bloom when they damn well please.

Where I live, even time
tries to take it all back:
pentimenti of stalk and thorn

and a penance of ice on everything
that once spoke lush or scarlet.

∼

On that very day, boomed Isaiah
via the booming preacher in our pulpit,
people will throw to the moles and to the bats
their idols of silver and gold,
what their own hands have made—
and I blanched in my Sunday petticoat,
precociously doomed.

Until the devil let me dream of topaz
and rubies stockpiled in pockets,
of wild words hidden
on the tips of tongues.

∼

Why should a simile give solace?
Why should strokes of yellow thrill
against a muddled ground?

Even February and its little ice age
can't undo the certainty of aconite
pushing through the shrunken snow like—
like what?

Spring's paparazzi.
Smidgens of heresy.
Hair triggers of hope.

Three

Tantrum, with Mistletoe

I've tried, like a peony, to explain myself
in a hundred dark petals or less.
I've been clear as the insatiable hands of the rain.
I've been Rachmaninoff and ragweed, cornflowers and castanets,
sunset swollen behind me like a red crescendo.
Yes, I've worn my heart up my sleeve. And Lord knows
I've been love's bull's-eye—
Saint Sebastiana of the Backslid Baptists.

Now snow mutes the buds and the barbed wire,
and you're out there somewhere, too, with your hot
blood and your cold shoulder, with your boots
finding fault with the garrulous white. But, honey,
what good's the last word if it just gets you gone?

I've coaxed the coals back into flame, uncorked
a sweetness even you can't argue with, and tacked up this truce
I scavenged for the doorjamb. Why don't you
come on in, and give me the slip
of your tongue? Why don't you put your mouth
where your moody heart is?

Duet for Ecclesiastes and Dutch Weather

1

The wind blows to the south and goes around to the north,
round and round goes the wind, saith the Preacher.

But *everybody's* talking this winter about the weather—
prophets, wise guys, whiners, winners.
Back home, they've named new species of storm
and concocted snowy synonyms for Apocalypse,
while the warmest winter in an eon is happening here
in a language I can't catch and that Google garbles:

This morning, one time shining in the east even the sun.
In the west, the clouds, and by noon, the light may rain.

2

Home is where the windswept heart was.

Here, it hopes to live within its means:
no debts or debtors, no trespassing either way,
and the squares on the tacked-up calendar
pristine as Dutch windows. But what if *the eye is* still
not satisfied with seeing, or the ear filled with hearing,
and what has been is what will be?

Each morning, when I hoist the heavy drapes, the high
clear pane reframes the question in cobalt
and a rush of North Sea cloud.

3

Everything else in this city knows what to do:
the trams clanging in perfect pitch, the canals
and their civilized water, the bijou bridges,
the flock and veer of bikes, precise as swallows.

Even the hothouse blooms in buckets,
hue by hue on the street corner.
Even the lager in the café glass
and the herring on thick ice at the fish stand.

Even the rumble of winter thunder.
Even the hail throwing its hissy fit.

4

Last night draw the rains from Belgium. In the course
of the night they left the country, though there is a new mood
emerged along the west coast, from which

a shrike flies in with the wind to my skinny yard,
skewers a mole in the fence-top flower box,
and plucks its muscles out among the crocus.

My neighbor can see this, too, from her identical
window, if she's watching. Who is my neighbor?
That woman who urged us as she kept the taxi waiting
to employ all four of our front door locks.

5

The poor will always be among us, even in the rich museum.
There, light singles out and saves a man
with the battered gleam of a pewter cup,
and soothes a ragged child with a tad of ochre
and the crusty likeness of bread.

If others still hunger and thirst in this humane city,
it's impossible to see them.
Though I have seen the naked—shades
darker than the Dutch, and in glass stalls
in the backside shadow of the oldest church.

6

This, I heard a tourist tell her husband, stumped
before the triptych, *is The Annunciation. And this
The Nativity. And this The Rest on the Flight to Europe.*

And this is what I've come for: the gilt gone,
and Flemish windows flung open to let in the light.

Behind each holy foreground, another tiny tour de force
of reeds, swans, gleaners, horsemen, spires.
Then an exhalation of white. Then indigo
striding more and more boldly away
from every earthly thing that painter knew.

7

*Next week have depressions eat mainly Scandinavia,
while a high-pressure nuclear southwest of Ireland
tries to keep the weather in our area—*

but if I'm reading right between the isobar lines,
it's just *to everything there is a season*, etcetera:
lows to the north, highs to the west, and in the middle

of the night sometimes a moon so merciful
it ransoms with silver every ripple, lock, and edge.

And sometimes a mood so black
there is nothing in heaven for a streetlight to blot out.

8

Big books on a small shelf, light from a wide window,
and no phone, no promises to keep.
Then a flier's pushed through the mail slot:
"Africa meets Amsterdam! Hijab meets hip-hop!
Since you're our neighbors, we thought we'd invite you!"

Who *else* are my neighbors? Some I recognize
from paintings: the cheeky maid at the check-out;
the tavern drunk turned frizzled pothead; the lovesick girl
on the tram frowning down at secrets
sent in air and hidden in her cagey hand.

9

Spring weather remains steadfast. A weak depression
in the immediate vicinity of the Netherlands
grabs his stuff, and the temperature takes a walk.

As do I, dodging locals sunning on every stretch
of canal-side brick that could conceivably be *café.*
But this ain't Paris: it's big beer, all round.

No one frets the lavish heat might mean Antarctica
is shrugging off its cold shoulder. They've flirted
here with luxury and sea level for centuries—and got
the dams, dikes, and Calvinism to prove it.

10

You can't count on good weather even at the Judgment.
All that light in the east stirs up thick thunderheads,
and not just beneath the Lord's left hand above the horny
hags of Hell: even the saved hurry out of graves
to beat the downpour.

But my favorite angel's in no rush.
He escorts his handsome catch into a heavenly line,
his hand firm on the other's naked ass. Innocent?
Hard to tell from his perfect face. Though he does gaze back,
above the routed and raptured and over a feathery shoulder,
to a past in which I seem to stand.

11

Possible that there is a temporary gray morning.
The weather is tentative, characterized
by lots of cloud and rain (rain).

        And I know how that feels,
the drab reviser in the brain fussing,
vanity, vanity, vanity of vanities . . .

Then I think of Clara Peeters.
Among her lush epitomes of lemon and slick fish,
she carved her name with paint onto a knife blade.
And on a quiet inch of the Golden Age's
finest pewter lid, she caught her cloud-lit face.

12

There is nothing better for mortals than to eat and drink
        and find enjoyment in their toil.
Light is sweet, and it is pleasant for the eyes to see the sun.

—Today we have to wait for the sun. Tomorrow the sun shines a lot,
        but still mostly cloudy watery veil hurt by some fields
in the morning. The rest of the week taps the back of a very
        different tune, making it ideal weather to tackle on a terrace—

or to douse the drapes, lug my duffle to the *Luchthaven*,
and head back home against the jet stream,
30,000 feet above the blue oblivion

and every possible April.

Vernal Knowledge

Some like it hot:
the mercury in stilettos and March flaunting
what it usually wants—loud
tulips among the stricken crocuses, blurts of green
from the tip of every twig, magnolias talking
pink trash to the wind, and nobody saving up
anything for summer.

But I like it shy:
snowdrops and inklings and crimson hints.
A flash of oriole.
A flush of bloom in the maple.
And the orchard, trusting through slow degrees, till each bud
shivers out the light it dreamed up in darkness
in the silent cell of itself.

"The Centuries Have a Way
of Being Male—"

but you wouldn't know that from this room: a mother
at the heart of every canvas, every square
of gold-besotted wood. She rests on thrones
or ruins or thresholds, patient
with whatever is in season—poverty or pomp.
Martyrs crowd in, brandishing, like inept Magi,
their lousy karma and bad luck charms.
A rich man begs, small as a terrier at her knee,
trying to shrink his way into paradise.
And Joseph fidgets at her shoulder—fiftyish
and still not ready for fatherhood. Or else he's entirely
out of the picture, like the god who knocked her up.
But she's got eyes only for the baby lounging
in her lap, who's got the whole world
of her breast in his tiny hands.

If she were the queen of earth, not merely
heaven, she'd stave off the Aves
and creeds, the canons and papal bulls, and linger
a few centuries more in this sunlit quiet—
where every urgent thing there is to say
can be said in milk.

Assorted Angels

If poets had patron saints, mine
would be Caedmon, tongue-tied cowherd
slinking out of the mead-hall bash
before the improviser's harp could circle round.
An angel found him later in the barnyard,
staring up at stars and humming to uncritical cows.
Only in that pungent quiet could an angel ever goad him
to lovely, thick, alliterative lines in praise of his workman God—
the Roofer nailing down each black and shining shingle of the sky.

Once, I leaned out of my study's second-story window
to sing the praises of an actual roofer.
I'd been spying, watching him size up, saw,
snug each cedar shake into eccentric eaves.
He'd fiddle till the pieces fit, each line aligned.
Inspired, I called him *Comrade,* and he laughed,
though I could tell he'd brush my insight off
the second I turned my back.
If poets had Devil's Advocates, I'd take him for mine.

Needing the Baroque

Rubens, I repent.
For years I had eyes only for conscientious Eves,

for thin northern hips and rumination
and the prim logic of a pared-down paradise—

apple, Adam, snake, a sprig of aftermath,
a second thought ripening inches above their heads.

I snubbed your operatic Eden, glimpsed it
through a threshold and walked on by!

Now I'd trade a century of gilt
for your free-range genesis, where everybody else

seems to have gotten to the fruit first:
fur, fin, plume, and slither.

Adam can't guess what's put the suave
in the stallion, the grin on the crocodile,

but Eve has her hunches. Reaching up
for the high-branch help of a boa,

she plucks what perfection still craves—
her skin a prophecy of milk and honey,

and the breeze teasing a wisp of gold
across the plump crux of her new matter.

The Moon Rising

Sly old guru, Rorschach moon,
you're calling me again with your round riddle,
your paradox of Ohm and moan.
All day the sun was up on its soapbox, a Pollyanna
casting out the darkness in everybody else.
Now we're back at the window where we started—
me with my midnight weakness, and you
with your sleight-of-silver ministry
to anyone unguarded and alone.

Slow moon, you've lingered near the cloister and the dance hall,
laid your soft law down on wide and narrow beds.
You've faced yourself in ponds, thrown yourself
on the mercy of a moody sea. You've been the slick
Houdini of horizons, sliding out of each tight spot
the night has tried to trap you in.
What's left for me to misconstrue?

I'm tired of my mind and its whitewash,
tired of your low-light revelations.
And how will I find the dark forest if you keep
murmuring silky nothings to the trees?

Cold moon, unmake me
in your image. Pare me down
to the bleak beatitude, the black sum
of all you know for sure.

Aubade for the Muse

A flutter at the threshold—
and here you are, nothing between us

but a throw rug and a hothouse lily.
Rosy and rugged, you grin

like a man who's spent a thousand nights
with a thousand soft-skinned books.

Last time you breezed in,
you had more critiques than a prophet

workshopping the Israelites.
You said I needed more *original* sins.

You nixed my metaphor and left
my ode blundering into bloom

against the glistening odds of the frost.
Who let you back inside my dream?

Toned down in khakis and crewneck,
you settle on the couch and trot out

that old line about needing me
to "flesh out" your "big idea."

Who knows? Maybe soon—maybe even before
the alarm—you'll recant the rant

and the razzmatazz and give me what
you know I always want: your speechless

mouth on mine, making it all up.

Summer Songs in the Key of X

The closest thing to menace in this fresh,
shallow, well-intentioned cove
is the snout of a snapping turtle,
camouflaged as the tip of a crocodile cruising
too close to my thin-skinned dinghy.
Evolution seems, mostly, on my side this time.

Not so at dusk, when mosquitos rev
their exquisite engines in the reeds.

Does the shade tree ever long for the solace of shade?
Does the mercury ever hope to fall
out of love with the naked sun?
Does the smooth water wish
to mess up its mind with its own wake?

A biting fly scribbles its itchy fraction
of a decibel on the sweaty air.
I know what it's saying—taunts
for the flail and swish and swat.

And the loon, with that low loose vowel, croons
Here, here, here, we are to its identical mate.

But what does the full moon mean—
that whole note on a long leash
climbing up so far into the black arpeggio
that the only ones left who can hear it
are already gone?

Driftings at Anchor

The lake leaps up at the wind's will—
chop or williwaw or cat's paws—
then lies back down in an ecstasy of sky.
It doesn't seem to need a gospel truth.

And consider the thick-skinned lilies, waterproof
with rope roots, equipped for deluge or drought,
the tern in hunger-honed freefall, the Jesus Bugs
dimpling the tension with their high-tech feet.

Out here, only I have mind enough to know
I don't know my own mind,
to watch away the afternoon, my thoughts
stalled like stumped disciples.

Chattanooga, 1958: Perry Como on the record player
and me wide-eyed by a dark window.
Catch a falling star and put it in your pocket.

Last night, though, I could hardly stay awake,
stretched out on deck to watch—not stars
and nothing worth wishing upon—just
atmosphere and dust from a comet's trashy tail.

Wind and rumors of wind and, on the mast top,
the edgy vane pointing its finger.

From our berth, my skipper second-guesses
the barometer and argues for a gusty passage,
while I check vectors and charts, insisting
this is where we're safe: in another bight
snug in an archipelago of granite.

He tightens the sullen rigging; I riffle
the calm as I swim, as does the blue-winged teal
cruising the reeds with her peppy brood.

But what might those ridgetop pines be trying to tell us?
Their high limbs flail in a surge of semaphore
I can't translate, can't even fathom what
euphoria, dervish, alleluia, alarm
thunders beyond the bluff.

      ∿

Job provoked the whirlwind and got
Who has cut a channel for the torrents of rain,
and a way for the thunderbolt?
Who has put wisdom in the inward parts,
or given understanding to the mind?
Who can tilt the waterskins of the heavens?

We just get pop quizzes of lightning,
redundancies of rain.

      ∿

While I napped, something stormy left behind
that loose end of a rainbow dangling

from clouds like the frescoed shins and soles
of a just-launched Jesus.

And here I am again among the foreshortened pious,
gawking up for a greedy glimpse.

⁓

If we turned it on this morning, the radio
would reach all the way to the zealots
and bring back the bloody news,
chaos in the cause of paradise.

So we listen to kingfishers rattle
and splash in this backwater heaven—
deep mud for the anchor; smooth rock
for the ducklings too far out in the bay for the fox;
neon slime for the brown frog nestling
its belly in, then converting
to chartreuse.

⁓

Denouement of another night's cold front,
dawn of drizzle and mist and everything a sotto voce blue.

Nothing out here is ever black and white—
except that dapper bird afloat

on the silence, exact copy
after the long-lost original of *loon*.

⁓

I might have gazed all day at the mountain
and the blue-gold fetch from there to here.

But the wind shifted, and the boat swung
and gave me this stern-row view of a pine,

scruffy among the elegant spruce and cocky sumac.
How long had this been happening behind my back—

the shimmering pine in the water
shimmering up onto the actual pine

transfigured in its own shimmerings?

At the Equinox

Has the rain a father, or who has begotten the drops of dew?
—Job 38:28

From the car window, after the fog lifts,
the autumn fields flash with sudden flowers—

    like filigrees of mirror, like alloys of lace and light.

A weird miracle? Some brilliant, manic manna?
Until, of course, it's only *spiders*—ten thousand

    that have worked the dark with rigs of silk

to snag a fly and then, surprising themselves,
have step-fathered the dew.

    And so, for an odd hour, hunger

glistens in galaxies, sieved
from passing thoughts of lake and air.

NOTES

Kind of Blue

"devil strip": slang, in northeastern Ohio and particularly Akron, for the strip of grass between the sidewalk and the street.

"Delilahs": Judges 16.

"Lazarus": John 11:28–38.

Alberta Clipper

"Alberta Clipper": a high-speed storm that swoops down from Canada bringing cold to the Great Lakes region.

Woman in Blue Reading a Letter

Vermeer's painting by the same name is in the Rijksmuseum, Amsterdam.

Species of Idolatry

"small, dull painting": Dirck van Delen, *Iconoclasm in a Church*, 1630, in the Rijksmuseum.

"*Beeldenstorm*": the iconoclastic destruction that raged in the Netherlands over several months in 1566.

In Another Aftermath

The Massacre of the Innocents: one of two paintings on the subject by Cornelis van Haarlem. This version is in the Frans Hals Museum, Haarlem.

"this great confusion of naked child-killers": Karel van Mander, *Schilderboeck*, 1604.

Duet for Ecclesiastes and Dutch Weather

"saith the Preacher": Ecclesiastes I:I–II.

"glass stalls / in the backside shadow of the oldest church": prostitute windows around the Oude Kerk, Amsterdam.

"my favorite angel's in no rush": Lucas van Leyden, *The Last Judgment*, 1527, in the Museum de Lakenhal, Leiden.

"Then I think of Clara Peeters": See her *Still Life with Cheeses, Almonds, and Pretzels*, ca. 1615, in the Mauritshuis, Den Haag.

"*There is nothing better for mortals than to eat and drink / and find enjoyment in their toil. / Light is sweet, and it is pleasant for the eyes to see the sun*": Ecclesiastes 2:24 and 11:7.

"The Centuries Have a Way of Being Male—"

The title quotation is from Wallace Stevens, "The Figure of the Youth as Virile Poet," 1944.

Needing the Baroque

"your operatic Eden": Jan Brueghel the Elder and Peter Paul Rubens, *The Garden of Eden with the Fall of Man*, ca. 1615, in the Mauritshuis.

WISCONSIN POETRY SERIES

Ronald Wallace, Series Editor

(B) = Winner of the Brittingham Prize in Poetry
(FP) = Winner of the Felix Pollak Prize in Poetry
(4L) = Winner of the Four Lakes Prize in Poetry